Childhoods

of the

Presidents

Thomas Jefferson

Childhoods *of the* Presidents

John Adams

George W. Bush

Bill Clinton

Ulysses S. Grant

Andrew Jackson

Thomas Jefferson

John F. Kennedy

Abraham Lincoln

James Madison

James Monroe

Ronald Reagan

Franklin D. Roosevelt

Theodore Roosevelt

Harry S. Truman

George Washington

Woodrow Wilson

Thomas Jefferson

Joseph Ferry

Mason Crest Publishers
Philadelphia

Produced by OTTN Publishing, Stockton, New Jersey

Mason Crest Publishers
370 Reed Road
Broomall, PA 19008
www.masoncrest.com

First printing

1 3 5 7 9 8 6 4 2

Library of Congress Cataloging-in-Publication Data
Ferry, Joseph.
    Thomas Jefferson / Joseph Ferry.
        p.   cm.   (Childhood of the presidents)
    Summary: A biography of the third president of the United
    States, focusing on his childhood and young adulthood.
    Includes bibliographical references and index.
        ISBN 1-59084-271-5 (hc.)
    1. Jefferson, Thomas, 1743-1826—Juvenile literature. 2. Jefferson,
    Thomas, 1743-1826—Childhood and youth—Juvenile literature.
    3. Presidents—United States—Biography—Juvenile literature. [1.
    Jefferson, Thomas, 1743-1826—Childhood and youth. 2.
    Presidents.] I. Title. II. Series.
    E332.79.F48 2003
    973.4'6'092—dc21
    [B]   2002024401

Childhoods
of the
Presidents

Table of Contents

★*Introduction*★

Alexis de Tocqueville began his great work *Democracy in America* with a discourse on childhood. If we are to understand the prejudices, the habits and the passions that will rule a man's life, Tocqueville said, we must watch the baby in his mother's arms; we must see the first images that the world casts upon the mirror of his mind; we must hear the first words that awaken his sleeping powers of thought. "The entire man," he wrote, "is, so to speak, to be seen in the cradle of the child."

That is why these books on the childhoods of the American presidents are so much to the point. And, as our history shows, a great variety of childhoods can lead to the White House. The record confirms the ancient adage that every American boy, no matter how unpromising his beginnings, can aspire to the presidency. Soon, one hopes, the adage will be extended to include every American girl.

All our presidents thus far have been white males who, within the limits of their gender, reflect the diversity of American life. They were born in nineteen of our states; eight of the last thirteen presidents were born west of the Mississippi. Of all our presidents, Abraham Lincoln had the least promising childhood, yet he became our greatest president. Oddly enough, presidents who are children of privilege sometimes feel an obligation to reform society in order to give children of poverty a better break. And, with Lincoln the great exception, presidents who are children of poverty sometimes feel that there is no need to reform a society that has enabled them to rise from privation to the summit.

Does schooling make a difference? Harry S. Truman, the only twentieth-century president never to attend college, is generally accounted a near-great president. Actually nine— more than one fifth—of our presidents never went to college at all, including such luminaries as George Washington, Andrew Jackson and Grover Cleveland. But, Truman aside, all the non-college men held the highest office before the twentieth century, and, given the increasing complexity of life, a college education will unquestionably be a necessity in the twenty-first century.

Every reader of this book, girls included, has a right to aspire to the presidency. As you survey the childhoods of those who made it, try to figure out the qualities that brought them to the White House. I would suggest that among those qualities are ambition, determination, discipline, education— and luck.

—ARTHUR M. SCHLESINGER, JR.

Thomas Jefferson's self-designed tombstone. The epitaph, which he also wrote, mentions his three proudest accomplishments: writing the Declaration of Independence and the Statute of Virginia for Religious Freedom, and founding the University of Virginia.

Origins of a Great American

*T*he *epitaph* on his tombstone, which he wrote himself, said simply, "Here was buried, Thomas Jefferson, Author of the Declaration of American Independence, of the Statute of Virginia for Religious Freedom, and Father of the University of Virginia." These were the three accomplishments of which Thomas Jefferson was proudest, and for which he wanted future generations to remember him. Even if these deeds were all that he had accomplished in his 83 years, they would have marked him as one of the great figures in American history.

Yet Jefferson accomplished quite a bit more. He was an author, an inventor, and a self-taught architect. He served as governor of Virginia and as U.S. secretary of state and vice president. He won election as the third president of the United States and doubled the size of the young nation through the Louisiana Purchase. In short, Jefferson could claim achievements enough for several lifetimes.

Thomas Jefferson entered the world in 1743, on April 13 (April 2 in the Old Style or Julian calendar then in use in the American colonies). The house in which he was born stood in the wilderness of the Virginia *colony*. Called Shadwell, after the district in London where his mother grew up, the Jefferson home wasn't like the great mansions built by rich *plantation* owners of that time. Instead it was a simple, four-room wooden structure. But the house stood on a sturdy stone foundation, the rooms were large and open, the living space was comfortable, and the Jefferson family loved it.

Peter Jefferson, Thomas's father, was one of the first settlers to move into the western part of the Virginia colony. His family had come from Wales and had worked hard to succeed in the new land of America. Peter Jefferson was a big, strong man. He was very smart, too. He liked to read and he worked as a *surveyor*, drawing maps.

Thomas's mother, Jane, came from the wealthy Randolph family, which was important in Virginia society. A warm and friendly woman, she loved to write.

Thomas's two big sisters, Jane and Mary, were delighted when their red-haired baby brother was born. They did their best to help care for him.

In 1743, few settler families lived in the area. Only a few farms dotted the forestland. It was so close to the *frontier* that Native Americans sometimes camped near the house and visited Thomas's father, who was known for his friendliness.

The area where Thomas Jefferson was born was called the Piedmont, which means "at the foot of the mountain." The Jefferson home was just east of the Blue Ridge Mountains.

The beauty of Shadwell and the love he knew there stayed with Thomas forever. Throughout his life, he kept

The schoolhouse at the Tuckahoe plantation, where Thomas Jefferson began his formal education at age five.

coming back to the Piedmont, as the area east of the Blue Ridge Mountains was called. In fact, it was there, on a hill overlooking a beautiful river, that he built Monticello, the magnificent home he designed himself.

Thomas was only two when the family left Shadwell. It was a sad move but one that had to be made after William Randolph, Mrs. Jefferson's cousin and Mr. Jefferson's best friend, died suddenly. The two men had promised to look after the other's family in the event one of them passed away. Not long before, Mr. Randolph's wife had also died.

The four Randolph children were alone in the world. They needed someone to look after them and to manage the huge Randolph estate, known as Tuckahoe. Everyone agreed that the hard-working Peter Jefferson was a good choice for the job.

But there was no way Mr. Jefferson could live at Shadwell and also take care of Tuckahoe. The two plantations were 70 miles apart, and it took three days to travel that distance on horseback. There was another good reason for the Jeffersons to move to Tuckahoe: Shadwell was much too small for a family that now included two adults and eight children.

Living at his new home was fun for young Thomas Jefferson. A big house, Tuckahoe featured several bedrooms, a large parlor, and a dining room. There was enough room for many people, and guests visited often.

All through the years the Jeffersons remained at Tuckahoe there were formal dinners, hunting parties, and lively dances in the mansion parlor. Many of Virginia's most respected citizens visited frequently. The activities at Tuckahoe were an important part of young Thomas's education. Just by living on the plantation he learned good manners, how to dance and eat properly, and how to behave in company—skills considered essential for a gentleman of the time.

Thomas was just one of many children growing up on the estate. To make sure they all received a good education, Mr. Jefferson hired a teacher to run a schoolroom. The teacher held classes in a small house near the mansion.

Even with two plantations to manage, Peter Jefferson kept a close eye on his son's schooling. When Thomas was five years old he began classes with his sisters and cousins. They learned arithmetic, reading, and especially penmanship. Clear handwriting was considered the sign of a good education at the time. Like other students, Thomas spent many hours dipping his goose-quill pen into a small inkbottle and practicing his letters. But he didn't always write on paper. One day, he wrote his name on a schoolroom wall. Visitors today can still see the signature on the wall at Tuckahoe.

Since there weren't any public libraries at the time, Thomas was fortunate that his father had a collection of more than 20 books. By the time he was six, the boy had read all the books once and was starting on them again.

Thomas attended the school at Tuckahoe for four years, learning reading, writing, and a small amount of arithmetic. He loved books, and he wrote down his thoughts about many things. But he didn't like to speak in front of the class. He would get nervous and speak so softly that his voice could barely be heard. Even as an adult Thomas Jefferson would avoid public speaking whenever possible.

If he had learned only to read and write, Thomas would still have received as much education as most Virginians of that time. But Peter Jefferson wanted more for his oldest son. He knew his son was a bright boy.

Even as a youngster, Thomas was interested in many subjects and kept careful records of everything that caught his attention. He wrote down the names of the birds, plants, and animals he saw. He even listed the names of different insects in his notebooks.

Thomas also learned the skills that a colonial gentleman needed to know. He was taught to shoot and ride well, and not just for the fun of it. Hunting wild animals put food on the table, and riding a horse was the only way to travel. In many parts of Virginia it was impossible to use a carriage because there were no roads.

A Father's Lessons

*A*fter seven years living at Tuckahoe, the Jeffersons were able to move back to Shadwell when Thomas was nine. The Randolph children had grown up and were able to take care of themselves and the property. They no longer needed a *guardian* to look after them.

Even though the family moved back to Shadwell, Thomas remained close to Tuckahoe in a boarding school run by Rev. William Douglas, a *clergyman* from Scotland. Douglas was the preacher at Dover Creek Church, five miles from Tuckahoe. His small school stood next to the church. Thomas lived at the school for four years. During that time he learned several languages, including Latin and Greek, and continued his studies in English and mathematics. The math he learned proved of great value in Thomas's adult life. As a young man he used mathematics when he worked as a land surveyor and, later, when he laid out the designs for Monticello.

Slavery was an accepted part of life in the Virginia of Thomas Jefferson's boyhood. As an adult Jefferson came to recognize that slavery did grave harm—to slaves as well as their masters—yet he remained a slaveholder until his death.

The subject Mr. Douglas taught best was French. Thomas learned to read, write, and speak the language very well. Years later, Thomas Jefferson would play an important role in the relationship between France and America, first as a *diplomat* and later when he became president. Being able to speak to the French in their language was a big help.

Thomas spent his school holidays and vacations at either Tuckahoe or Shadwell. Being away from school meant freedom and a chance to play. It also meant good meals, not the small pieces of cold meat pie that students got at Mr. Douglas's dinner table.

But for most of the school year, Thomas lived at Douglas's home, and in return for room and board and schooling for his son Peter Jefferson paid 19 pounds a year. This was more money than many colonists earned in a year. Still, it did not buy the kind of comforts to which Thomas had become accustomed at Shadwell or Tuckahoe.

When he wasn't in school, Thomas helped out his mother, father, and sisters on the plantation. The hardest work on the plantation, as Thomas could see, was performed by black slaves. Slaves took care of the horses and drove the wagons. Slaves planted the gardens and weeded the fields. Slaves picked the tobacco and corn and cotton. Slaves cooked the food and cleaned the house. A slave's children were slaves, too. Slave children didn't go to school—they worked along with their parents.

Thomas also saw white children copying the way their parents and other white adults treated slaves. If an adult ordered a slave about in a rude way, the child learned to do the

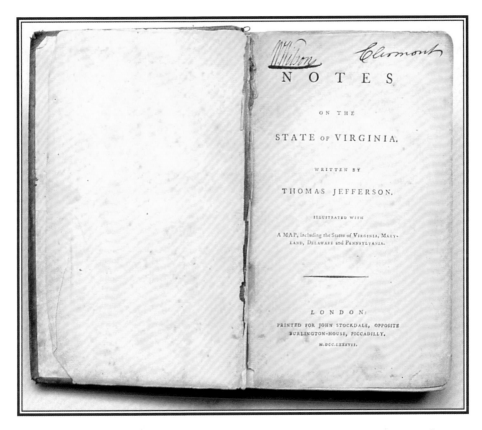

Jefferson's *Notes on the State of Virginia* contained observations on the natural history and political and social life of his home state—including some remarkable insights on the evils of slavery. On slavery he wrote with a sense of foreboding, "I tremble for my country when I reflect that God is just: that his justice cannot sleep forever."

same. This situation struck Thomas as wrong, and he remembered it all his life, writing about it in his book *Notes on the State of Virginia*. And yet, even as he wrote about how slavery *degraded* slaves and corrupted the "manners and morals" of slave owners, the adult Thomas Jefferson had more than 100 slaves working his fields.

During his childhood Thomas had plenty of slaves around to do whatever he needed, whenever he wanted. But his father taught Thomas something else. "Never ask another," Peter Jefferson said, "to do for you what you can do for yourself." It's not known whether the young Thomas Jefferson saw this advice as somewhat odd, coming as it did from a slaveholder. What is known is that the boy greatly respected his father.

During school vacations, Thomas sometimes took short trips with his father, who taught him to ride a horse, shoot a gun, and hunt wild turkeys and deer. He also learned from his father how to paddle a canoe on the river. The two often went into the wilderness west of the Allegheny Mountains. Mr. Jefferson, who was a part-time surveyor, liked exploring the forestlands. He drew maps of mountain passes and waterways and charted territory for possible settlements. Peter Jefferson was fascinated by the size of the continent. It seemed to stretch out forever to the west.

Together with his surveying partner, Joshua Fry, Mr. Jefferson made the first map of the whole colony of Virginia, the largest of the American colonies. The two men shared a great dream, and as he listened to their conversations, Thomas found himself caught up in their excitement. The two men had heard stories that there was a river in the west, with branches that flowed out into the Pacific Ocean. No one knew if these stories were true. But

Thomas never forgot his father's dream of finding a route to the Pacific Ocean. He made it come true when he was president of the United States and commissioned the Lewis and Clark Expedition. Meriwether Lewis and William Clark led the group that did find a passage from the center of the continent to the Pacific coast.

Peter Jefferson and Joshua Fry wanted to be the first ones to find out. Their plan was to form a party of explorers and surveyors and head west into the unknown territory. They hoped to find routes to the Pacific.

Though he dreamed of someday exploring the continent, Peter Jefferson was no rootless wanderer. He had established himself as a leader in the Virginia colony. At different times he served as sheriff, judge, justice of the peace, and member of the Virginia House of Burgesses (the group of men who made laws for the colony). For this service and for his intelligence, Thomas Jefferson looked up to his father.

It must have been very difficult on the boy, then, when his father died suddenly in August 1757. Peter Jefferson was only 49 and had never been sick, so the death came as quite a shock. Thomas Jefferson, just 14 years old, found himself with no man to model his life after, no man to guide him. What's more, by this time he had six sisters and a brother, and he felt that it was his responsibility to take care of them. He desperately missed his father. He felt alone in the world.

In his will, Peter Jefferson left something to each of his children. As the oldest son, however, Thomas received the most, including 7,500 acres of land, 200 hogs, 70 head of cattle, and 25 horses. Thomas would be expected to help his *siblings* with this inheritance. Knowing how much learning meant to Thomas, his father had also left him his desk, his bookcase, his math instruments, and his collection of books. He also willed to his son a personal slave.

A Boy of Many Interests

Even though he was smart and a hard worker, at 14 Thomas was far too young to run the family estate. Five men, named by Peter Jefferson in his will, were to advise Jane Jefferson for the next seven years. They would manage the estate for Mrs. Jefferson and her children until Thomas reached age 21. Then, in accordance with the will, he would assume responsibility for managing the estate. At that time he would also receive many additional slaves and more than 2,100 acres of land.

One of the first decisions the guardians made was that Thomas should continue his education closer to home. He was sent to Rev. James Maury's small school about 14 miles from Shadwell. Although he lived at the log schoolhouse, he was now able to come home regularly.

Mr. Maury was a serious man and an excellent teacher. He knew Greek and Latin far better than Thomas's previous

An actor portrays Thomas Jefferson practicing his violin. From the time he first picked up a violin around age 14, Thomas was an enthusiastic player, devoting several hours each day to practicing the instrument.

teacher, Mr. Douglas. He also taught *geology*, *botany*, and other natural sciences. And he had a library of more than 400 books. During the next two years, Thomas began reading about such subjects as philosophy and government. Mr. Maury encouraged his new student to think about the relationship between people and their government, a topic that 18th-century European philosophers had been exploring. Who should make laws? Only men who owned land or all the people? Maury helped Thomas think about laws and rights and justice.

Going to school took up only part of Thomas's days. The tall, thin, redheaded teenager had endless energy, which he used in dozens of ways. He was a fine rider who delighted in having horse races with his cousins and schoolmates.

Hunting was another of his favorite activities, and he kept an exact record of every animal he shot. He listed its weight, size, color, and every other fact he considered worthwhile. When he shot a tree squirrel on a hunting trip, he would record how much it weighed. He wanted to learn whether red, gray, and black squirrels all weighed the same. It was typical of young Thomas Jefferson to pay close attention to these details, and to write them down. This was a practice that stayed with him for the rest of his life.

Thomas Jefferson devised a plan for American money that was based on the number 10. He divided a dollar into 100 pennies or 10 dimes.

Thomas also began taking violin lessons during his years at Mr. Maury's school, and playing the instrument became another lifelong passion. From the first day he

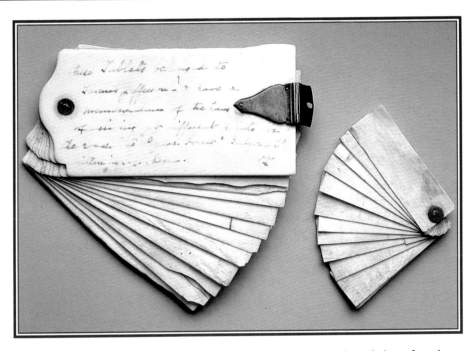

Two of the ivory tablets that Thomas Jefferson carried with him for the purpose of recording, in pencil, his thoughts and observations. Later he would transfer the information into his permanent notebooks, erasing and reusing the ivory tablets.

picked up the violin, Thomas practiced it two or three hours every day. Whether learning to play a musical instrument, riding his horse, studying nature or French or math, Thomas Jefferson did it with all his heart.

While he was living and studying with Mr. Maury, Thomas met Dabney Carr, who would become his best friend. Dabney's horse was much faster than the one Thomas rode. But one day, Thomas bet that his friend couldn't beat him in a horse race on February 30. Days passed and at the end of the month, Dabney realized he'd been tricked. There was no way he could beat Thomas on the 30th—there are only 28 days in February!

A view of Monticello, the beautiful estate house Thomas Jefferson designed and built on a hilltop near Charlottesville, Virginia. Architecture was but one of Jefferson's many interests, which also included music, the natural sciences, and philosophy.

Thomas and Dabney frequently took their horses out for long rides together, often chasing after deer. They also liked to sit under a huge oak tree on the little mountain near the school and talk seriously about what they wanted to be when they grew older. The friends made a promise to each other: when one of them died, the other would make sure he was buried under the oak tree.

In the fall of 1759, Dabney told Thomas he was leaving Mr. Maury's school. In the spring, Dabney would be going off to study at William and Mary College in Williamsburg, Virginia. It was a good college, but Dabney was interested in more than schooling. He told Thomas that Williamsburg was an exciting place to live. There were dances, dinners, parties, plays, and concerts. Dabney said the best and smartest people in Virginia went there.

Right away, Thomas wanted to go to Williamsburg with his friend. He hoped his guardians would give him permission. To get that permission, he knew his request had to make good sense. So he carefully thought out his reasons for wanting to go to William and Mary.

First, he wrote in a letter, many young people visited him at Shadwell. This kept him from his studies. It also cost a great deal of money to feed and take care of those guests. If he were away at college, his reasoning went, the estate would not have to spend so much money entertaining company. Second, he informed his guardians, in Williamsburg he would meet people who would be of help to him in the future. Finally, he pointed out, he could take more advanced studies in Greek, Latin, and mathematics.

Thomas's guardians agreed that he would benefit a great deal from going to college and living in Williamsburg. As a future gentleman and landowner, he would be expected to take part in governing the colony of Virginia. Therefore, he needed to learn more about the entire colony, not just his area. He also needed to participate in adult society. The guardians knew that only by living in the capital of Virginia would Thomas encounter all kinds of situations and people. They granted their permission.

4

During his years at the College of William and Mary, Thomas Jefferson (portrayed here by an actor) developed a rigorous daily routine of work, study, and exercise that he would follow for the rest of his life. He rose at dawn and went to bed at 2 A.M.

An Education
in Williamsburg

Virginia colonists from Jefferson's time considered Williamsburg a large city. It had about 200 houses and 1,500 permanent residents. For a boy from the frontier, it was an awesome sight. The town had unpaved streets laid out in straight lines, which ran east-west and north-south. No street in Williamsburg curved or even went off at an angle.

Thomas Jefferson was almost 17 when he arrived in Williamsburg with his slave, Jupiter, also 17. It was the spring of 1760 and the capital was in the midst of its busiest season. The Virginia *legislature*, called the House of Burgesses, met in Williamsburg every spring. (Burgess was the name for an elected representative in Virginia.)

William and Mary College was not like the colleges of today. It was actually divided into four schools. There was a grammar school for boys 14 and younger. The school Thomas Jefferson entered was the school of philosophy. There was also a school of divinity, for students who wanted to be clergymen. Finally, there was a school for American Indians. The college had about 100 students and six teachers.

At first Thomas was disappointed in his classes. Because he

had read so much and learned so well in his earlier schools, he was way ahead of his classmates. He also found it hard to keep his mind on his studies. He wanted to be part of the excitement going on in the town. Soon, he and Dabney Carr were enjoying the nonstop social life around them.

Thomas made many good friends among the people of Williamsburg. They liked the tall, red-haired, freckle-faced young man. He had fine manners, danced very well, and played the violin superbly. He was invited to many homes for dinner. Thomas spent much of his money at the neighborhood coffeehouse, dancing, singing, and flirting with the beautiful young women of Williamsburg. He wasn't good at telling jokes, but his gray-green eyes were warm and cheerful, and he was considered one of the most likeable men in the city.

But all that fun came at a price. In his first year at college, Thomas spent more money than he should have. Because he was fairly wealthy, he was able to buy things at stores on *credit* just by signing his name. A bill would be sent to him later. His worn and rugged clothes were not fine enough for Williamsburg, so he had a whole new wardrobe made, including silk stockings and fancy hats. He ordered fine saddles, bridles, and other supplies for the horses he kept at a stable near the school. As a result, he found himself owing a lot of money by the end of the school year.

Thomas didn't have enough money to cover his bills. He had to write to one of his guardians for help. But he was so ashamed of wasting money that he asked that the bills be paid from his part of the family estate. He felt that his brother and sisters shouldn't have to share the cost of his foolishness.

A view of the Governor's Palace in Williamsburg. Thomas Jefferson spent many evenings dining at the palace and discussing politics and philosophy with Francis Fauquier, the English governor of the Virginia colony.

In his second year at William and Mary, Thomas had little time for foolishness. His schoolwork was more demanding than it had been the first year. He took long and detailed notes as he listened to his teachers, and he also wrote down many notes when he read books. He believed that if he wrote down the information, he would remember it better. And if he did forget something, he could always look at his papers to refresh his memory.

Three very different—and very important—men took an interest in Thomas that year because each saw something special in him. One was William Small, his math, science, and philosophy teacher. Small became like a second father. He

Many stores lined the main street of Williamsburg. There was a wigmaker's shop, a gunsmith's shop, and a candlemaker's store. Next to the jeweler's shop was the Raleigh Tavern. College students spent idle hours there talking, drinking, and playing cards.

introduced Thomas to the second man who would take a special interest in the youth: George Wythe, a brilliant lawyer who took Thomas under his wing. The third man was Francis Fauquier, the English governor of Virginia.

These well-respected men invited Thomas to become a part of their group, and a new world opened up to him. Many evenings, Thomas dined on oysters and wild duck at the Governor's Palace, where he found out more about politics, philosophy, and science in a few months than he had learned in all his previous years.

Dr. Small, the new head of the school of philosophy, saw that young Thomas Jefferson was unusually intelligent and needed only to be wisely guided. When Thomas was tempted to go downtown for a horse race or some other excitement, Dr. Small would suggest they take a long walk to discuss Greek thinkers or some other subject. Thomas wanted to please Dr. Small, so he almost always went along. Dr. Small made sure that his pupil read widely in poetry, philosophy, history, Greek, Latin, French, and science. He also encouraged Thomas to use the equipment in the William and Mary laboratory.

The college had the best-equipped laboratory in the colonies. It contained *barometers*, telescopes, and many other scientific instruments. Thomas's scientific studies paved the way for his later success as an inventor. Among his inventions were a mechanical letter-writer, a dumbwaiter (a kind of elevator for moving things from one floor in a building to another), a clock that told both the time and the day of the week, a more efficient plow, and a furnace that heated an entire house with warm air.

During his second year at college, Thomas developed patterns of work and study that he would follow for the rest of his life. He awoke every morning at dawn to begin studying. The day was divided into class hours, meals, more study, exercise, and still more study before he went to bed at 2 A.M.

Dabney Carr and others were amazed at the change in Thomas's habits. He started each day by putting his feet in a tub of cold water that Jupiter brought. He believed this kept him from getting sick. It must also have helped wake him up!

Thomas also spent three to four hours each day practicing his violin. Despite all that work, he found time to be with friends, attend an occasional party, and take part in a *string quartet*. At about this point in his life, he began to keep a daily diary. In it, he noted how his days progressed and what he accomplished. This was his way of making sure that he didn't fall into lazy habits.

Thomas even found time to fall in love for the first time. Her name was Rebecca Burwell, and she was one of the most beautiful women in Williamsburg. Thomas wrote notes to Dabney about the "beautiful R.B." and composed romantic poems about her. But when he actually tried to talk to Rebecca, he usually managed little more than a few stammered sen-

George Wythe, one of the most famous lawyers in Virginia, took a special interest in the bright and promising Thomas Jefferson, who would eventually leave William and Mary to study law under him. Pictured here is the interior of the Wythe House.

tences. To his great surprise, Rebecca married someone else.

After his second year at William and Mary, 19-year-old Thomas Jefferson left college to study law with George Wythe, who was one of the most important lawyers in Virginia. Thomas's friends considered him lucky to be given such an opportunity.

There were no law schools in those days. Someone who wanted to become a lawyer had to work for an attorney, read law books, and learn as much as possible. Then, after a few years, the young clerk would be tested by a group of attorneys. If he did well in this examination, he was accepted into the practice of law.

The five years that Thomas spent studying law with Mr. Wythe proved to be extremely important in his future, and in the future of the country. In addition to learning as much as he could

Dabney Carr died one day while Thomas was away from Shadwell. Remembering their boyhood promise to each other, Thomas had Dabney's coffin dug up and placed in a grave under the big oak tree where they had sat so often as youngsters.

about the current laws of England and the colonies, Thomas studied the history and development of English law. He thought about the relationship between rulers and the people they ruled. Should citizens always obey the laws their rulers created? What if the laws themselves were unjust?

This was a serious matter to the people who lived in colonial America. It was, in fact, one of the issues that led to the American Revolution.

Flanked by the other members of the drafting committee, Thomas Jefferson (center, with red vest) presents the Declaration of Independence to the Continental Congress. The document had taken him more than two weeks to write.

Patriot and President

One day in 1764, while he was studying law in Williamsburg, Thomas heard a speaker attack the policies of Great Britain and its king, who wanted to impose new taxes on the American colonists. The speech made Thomas think about the future of his country: should America remain loyal to Great Britain, or should it seek independence?

Back home at Shadwell, Thomas began to practice law. He also began to build a home of his own on land he had inherited from his father. It would stand at the top of a high hill, so he named it Monticello, which means "little mountain" in Italian.

Thomas Jefferson had never studied architecture, but he designed Monticello himself with the help of books from Europe. By the fall of 1770, a one-room redbrick building was finished. Thomas moved in with his books and violin while work continued on the main house.

That same year, he met Martha Wayles Skelton, the daughter of a lawyer in Williamsburg. She loved music as much as Thomas and accompanied him on the *harpsichord* when he played his violin.

This time Thomas was not too shy to declare his love. He proposed to Martha, and they were married at her home on New Year's Day, 1772. The Jeffersons' first child, a girl, was born in September of that year. They named her Martha after her mother.

Besides his family and Monticello, Thomas had another responsibility. He had been elected to represent his county in Virginia's House of Burgesses. This group of men helped the royal governor run the colony, but trouble was brewing with Great Britain.

Up north in Boston, colonists protesting a British tax dumped a load of tea into the harbor in December 1773. This event became known as the Boston Tea Party. The Virginia House of Burgesses supported the actions of their fellow Americans in Massachusetts. They proposed that *delegates* from all 13 colonies meet each year in a *congress* so they could discuss their common problems.

By the time the Second Continental Congress convened in Philadelphia in 1775, the first battles of the Revolutionary War had been fought in Massachusetts. Still, some delegates clung to the hope that the American colonies and Great Britain might yet *reconcile*.

By spring of the following year, that seemed impossible, and the Continental Congress decided to completely break away from England. The delegates needed a document that would make their case—a document to let fellow Americans, the British, and the rest of the world know why they had taken this course of action. They turned to Thomas Jefferson, one of the Virginia delegates. Although quiet during debates, he was one of the best writers at the Congress.

It took Thomas 17 days to write and rewrite the Declaration of Independence. He wanted to make sure every word and every sentence were just right. After he gave the finished draft to Congress, the members spent three more days going over it line by line. They changed a bit of the wording and cut some of what Thomas had included. Thomas didn't like this editing, but he didn't argue because his thoughts had not been changed.

At last, on July 4, 1776, Congress adopted the Declaration of Independence. Jefferson's powerful words still move people more than two centuries later: "We hold these truths to be self-evident, that all men are created equal, that they are endowed by their Creator with certain *unalienable* Rights, that among these are Life, Liberty and the pursuit of Happiness."

The Declaration listed the crimes of the British king and explained why Americans should fight for their freedom. It was one of the most important documents ever written in the United States—or the world.

When he returned to Virginia, Thomas urged the new state to enact several important laws. One, which was never passed, would end the slave trade. (Interestingly, Thomas knew that plantations such as Monticello couldn't be run without slave labor, and he continued to own slaves.) The other law, which Thomas began writing in 1777, was the Virginia Statute for Religious Freedom. When Virginia finally passed the law, it marked the first time a government had guaranteed religious freedom to its citizens and officially separated religion from

Charles M. Russell's *Lewis and Clark on the Lower Columbia* depicts an encounter between Native Americans and the expedition Thomas Jefferson sent to explore the Louisiana Purchase territory. Buying the huge territory from France, which doubled the size of the United States, was one of Jefferson's most important acts as president.

government control. Jefferson's statute served as a model for Article 1 of the Bill of Rights in the U.S. Constitution.

In 1779, when Thomas was elected governor of Virginia, the fighting in the Revolutionary War was taking place elsewhere. But then, a year later, a large British force landed near the capital of Richmond.

The British tried to capture Thomas, but he escaped just in

time. Soon afterward, the British were defeated at Yorktown. The United States had won its independence, and peace returned to Virginia.

Thomas decided to retire from public life when his term as governor was up. Back at Monticello, he enjoyed his farm, his family, his books, and his music. But his happiness didn't last long.

Over the years, Thomas and his wife had five children, but only two lived. Now, after giving birth to another child, Mrs. Jefferson got sick and died. Thomas was devastated. For three weeks he didn't even come out of his room.

Thomas grieved for six months before he became interested in life again. Then, in 1784, he accepted an assignment from Congress. He sailed to France, where he became a special *ambassador* in Paris.

When France exploded into revolution, President George Washington called Thomas home to America for a new assignment as secretary of state. Later, Thomas served as vice president under John Adams. Finally, in 1801 he was elected president of the United States.

On inauguration day, Thomas got up early and dressed in a heavy gray coat and green pants. He left his boardinghouse in the new capital city of Washington and walked by himself the two blocks to the Capitol Building, which was still under construction.

Thomas took his oath of office and gave a speech he had written himself. But only those people sitting in the first four rows of the audience could hear his words. He was still shy about speaking in public.

The White House was only one year old when Thomas Jefferson moved in. It was known then as President's House.

After the inauguration, Thomas moved into the White House by himself because his daughters had to stay in Virginia with their families. As president, Thomas did away with formal gatherings. Instead, he entertained with small private dinners. The table was round so no guest would sit in a more important place than another.

In 1804, Thomas ran for reelection and won easily. When his term ended in 1809, he returned to Monticello. His daughter Martha, the only one of his six children still living, joined him there with her family. Thomas loved to play with his 11 grandchildren.

When he was 75, Thomas began a new project. He had always believed in the importance of education, so he started a three-part school system for Virginia. There would be a free public elementary school for all children, a free high school within one day's ride of every teenager, and a state university in Charlottesville, near Monticello.

In 1825, the University of Virginia was completed. Thomas attended the opening ceremonies. He was proud of the school. But he was also worried. He had gone deep into debt and was in danger of losing Monticello, the home he loved so much.

To raise money to pay his bills, Thomas sold one of the things he loved most—his library. The United States Congress paid him $25,000 for almost 6,000 books. It was a lot of money but not enough to pay his debts. Thomas was afraid he would have to sell everything he owned. And that meant he would

Artist Thomas Sully painted this portrait of Thomas Jefferson in March 1821, when the former president was 77, living at Monticello, and working on plans for the University of Virginia.

have nothing to leave his family after he died.

When word of Thomas's troubles spread, people all across the country wanted to help. They couldn't believe such a thing was happening to the man who had meant so much to the young nation. Committees in New York, Philadelphia, Baltimore, and other cities raised thousands of dollars for him. Smaller gifts came from farms and villages.

The generosity meant much to Thomas. With Monticello saved, he could make his will and prepare to die in his beloved house.

By the end of June 1826, Thomas knew he didn't have much time left. But he was determined to live at least until July 4. It would be the 50th anniversary of the signing of the Declaration of Independence, and he wanted to see that day.

At night on the third of July, Thomas asked his doctor, "Is it the Fourth?"

"It soon will be," the doctor said, and Thomas smiled.

The next day, at a little past noon, he died.

CHRONOLOGY

1743 Thomas Jefferson is born on April 13 at his family's home, Shadwell, in western Virginia.

1757 Peter Jefferson, his father, dies.

1760 Enters the College of William and Mary in Williamsburg, Virginia.

1762 Graduates from college and begins to study law.

1770 Loses his first collection of books and notes in a fire that destroys Shadwell on February 1.

1772 Marries a widow, Martha Wayles Skelton, on January 1; first child, Martha, is born.

1775 Revolutionary War begins.

1776 Mother, Jane Randolph Jefferson, dies; Jefferson writes Declaration of Independence at Second Continental Congress in Philadelphia.

1778 Daughter Maria is born.

1779 Elected governor of Virginia.

1781 British surrender at Yorktown, Virginia.

1782 Daughter Lucy Elizabeth is born; wife, Martha, dies at age 33.

1789 George Washington is inaugurated as the first president of the United States.

1790 Jefferson accepts appointment as secretary of state.

1796 Elected vice president of the United States.

1801 Elected president of the United States.

1804 Daughter Maria dies.

1826 Thomas Jefferson dies at Monticello on July 4, the 50th anniversary of the adoption of the Declaration of Independence.

ambassador—an authorized messenger or representative.

barometer—an instrument for measuring air pressure.

botany—the study of plants.

clergyman—a minister.

colony—an area controlled by a distant nation.

congress—a formal meeting of delegates for discussion of, and sometimes action on, a question or issue.

credit—buying something and promising to pay for it later.

degrade—to lower in rank or status; to drag down the character or morals of; to corrupt.

delegates—representatives to a conference or convention.

diplomat—a person who represents his or her country in official matters in a foreign nation.

epitaph—words on a tombstone or grave in memory of the person buried there.

frontier—an area of land at the edge of territory that has not been settled or explored.

geology—the study of rocks.

guardian—a person who is put in charge of others who can't take care of themselves (often children).

harpsichord—a keyboard instrument whose strings are plucked by means of quills or picks.

legislature—a group of people who make laws.

plantation—an estate with a very large farm that usually harvests one main crop.

reconcile—to settle differences; to restore to friendship or harmony.

siblings—brothers and sisters.

string quartet—four people playing music on stringed instruments, usually two violins, a viola, and a cello.

surveyor—a person whose job is to measure land.

unalienable—not able to be surrendered or transferred.

FURTHER READING

Adler, David A. *Thomas Jefferson, Father of Our Democracy*. New York: Holiday House, Inc., 1987.

Ferris, Jeri Chase. *Thomas Jefferson, Father of Liberty*. Minneapolis, Minn.: Carolrhoda Books, Inc., 1998.

Ferry, Joseph. *The Jefferson Memorial*. Philadelphia: Mason Crest Publishers, 2003.

Jones, Veda Boyd. *Thomas Jefferson, Author of the Declaration of Independence*. Philadelphia: Chelsea House Publishers, 2000.

Marcovitz, Hal. *The Declaration of Independence*. Philadelphia: Mason Crest Publishers, 2003.

Sabin, Francene. *Young Thomas Jefferson*. Mahwah, N.J.: Troll Associates, 1986.

Severance, John B. *Thomas Jefferson, Architect of Democracy*. New York: Clarion Books, 1998.

- http://www.whitehouse.gov/history/firstladies/mj3.html
  A brief biography of Thomas Jefferson's wife, Martha

- http://www.nps.gov/inde/education/BIB.htm
  A bibliography of titles on the colonial, Revolutionary War, and early Federal eras

- http://www.loc.gov/exhibits/jefferson/jeffwest.html
  Pages that explore Thomas Jefferson's interest in the West, including the Louisiana Purchase and the Lewis and Clark expedition

- http://www.whitehouse.gov/history/presidents/tj3.html
  White House biography of Thomas Jefferson

- http://www.monticello.org
  Official website of Monticello

- http://memory.loc.gov/ammem/mtjhtml/mtjhome.html
  The Thomas Jefferson Papers at the Library of Congress

INDEX

INDEX

PICTURE CREDITS

Contributors

ARTHUR M. SCHLESINGER JR. holds the Albert Schweitzer Chair in the Humanities at the Graduate Center of the City University of New York. He is the author of more than a dozen books, including *The Age of Jackson*; *The Vital Center*; *The Age of Roosevelt* (3 vols.); *A Thousand Days: John F. Kennedy in the White House*; *Robert Kennedy and His Times*; *The Cycles of American History*; and *The Imperial Presidency*. Professor Schlesinger served as Special Assistant to President Kennedy (1961–63). His numerous awards include the Pulitzer Prize for History; the Pulitzer Prize for Biography; two National Book Awards; the Bancroft Prize; and the American Academy of Arts and Letters Gold Medal for History.

JOSEPH FERRY is a veteran journalist who has worked for several newspapers in Philadelphia and the surrounding suburbs. He has written several books for children, including *The American Flag*, *The Jefferson Memorial*, *The National Anthem*, and *The Vietnam Veterans Memorial*. Mr. Ferry lives in Sellersville, Bucks County, Pennsylvania, with his wife, three children, and two dogs.